10 Quick Tip Strategies to Enhance Classroom and Behavior Management

Dr. Michael S. Hubler, Ed.D.

& Lillian I. Hubler, C.D.A.

ISBN-13: 978-1512359732
ISBN-10: 1512359734

CONTENTS

ACKNOWLEDGMENTS

This book is written with sincere appreciation
to all the preschool teachers and staff who
serve our nation's children.

INTRODUCTION

CLASSROOM MANAGEMENT STRATEGIES & HELPFUL HINTS

Classroom Management - Issues

Classroom management college and professional development training is of the utmost importance. Research confirms this is the number one issue for new teachers. Studies reveal that poor classroom management skills and disruptive students are the two most significant barriers to their professional success.

Classroom Management – Definition

Classroom management is the actions teachers take to create an environment conducive to social, emotional, and academic learning. Effective classroom management is essential to successful teaching. *Prevention is the key to classroom management. It sets the stage for learning.*

Classroom Management for Teachers:

1. Teacher Attitude/Beliefs
   - Be aware of personal biases.
   - Acknowledge negative thoughts.
   - Believe all children can succeed.
   - Be self-aware of one's own cultural differences.

2. Interactions
- Greet all students at the door everyday as they enter the classroom.
- Create a climate of tolerance.
- Treat all members of the class with dignity, fairness, and respect.
- Provide students with opportunities to work with many people.
- Give feedback that is direct, immediate, authentic, and tactful.

3. Home/School Collaboration
- Learn about students' lives beyond the classroom.
- Understand that family structures vary.
- Maintain contact with the families based on students' needs.

4. Instruction
- Use direct and explicit instruction.
- Use the active voice in responding to students with performance feedback.
- Use cooperative learning groups.

5. Management System
- Emphasize prevention strategies.
- Develop rules and explicitly teach them.
- Emphasize the use of reinforcement-based strategies.
- Provide individualized corrective consequences.

Improving Your Practice

Following are strategies that teachers can easily implement as they begin to establish an effective classroom management plan and move away from an over-reliance on extrinsic rewards.

Sign Language Benefits

Benefits of using sign language with preschool children include:

- 2-sided brain activity that increases brain functioning
    - Visual right brain usage
    - Cognitive second language left brain usage
    - Creates additional connections or synapses in the brain
    - Creates higher IQ levels in Children
- A fun activity for child and parent/caregiver that reduces frustration and enhances bond between child and parent/caregiver
- Enhances vocabulary, pre-literacy concept recognition and understanding and reading skills
- Enhances fine motor coordination
- Enables children to control their hyperactive tendencies
- Boosts children's confidence and self-esteem
- Raises communication awareness and abilities

Classroom benefits of sign language include:

- Lowers children's noise levels in the classroom
- Reduces need for teachers to raise their voice
- Enables class to support special needs children
- Increases children's use of manners
- Sign language gets their attention better than the spoken word
- Children pay better attention, they have to look directly at you
- Increased ability to express themselves reduces instances of misbehavior
- Provides children the ability to express emotions

Dr. Marilyn Daniels thoughts on the benefits of sign language: The added benefits of signing derive in part from its unique status as both a visual and kinetic language. There are individual memory stores for each language a person knows, even at the initial stages of acquiring the second or third language. You intake sign with your eyes, using the right side of the brain. Then like any other language, sign is processed and stored in the brain's left hemisphere. This operation creates more synapses in the brain, adding to its growth and development. It also helps to establish two memory stores in the left hemisphere for language, one for English (or the native language) and one for ASL. So children who use both develop a built-in redundancy of memory, storing the same word in two formats in two places.

Furthermore, because visual cues are taken in with the right side of the brain while language engages the left using ASL activates both sides of the brain at once. In the same way that bilingual children develop greater brain function, users of sign language build more connections or synapses in the brain than those who use English alone and because of the kinetic component of sign language, the ASL brain benefits even more than the bilingual one because of the dual-hemisphere work. Babies using sign language are simply building more brain.

For a more in-depth analysis of this topic I suggest you consult my web site marilyndaniels.com or my book, *Dancing with Words: Signing for Hearing Children's Literacy*, where you will find additional information. I wish each of you and the children with whom you communicate much success in realizing the benefits of sign language.

Dr. Marilyn Daniels
Marilyn Daniels, Ph.D.
Associate Professor
Department of Speech
Communication
Penn State University

Quick Tip 1:
Developing Rules and Routines

Rules

Create four to six classroom rules that clearly specify appropriate behavior. Students should help in the creation of these rules. Write the rules using positive
language. Post at child height and refer to the rules as necessary.

Routines

Develop routines to provide direction about how different classroom tasks are accomplished. A classroom's practiced and rehearsed daily procedures are essential to effective classroom management.

Common routines and procedures include: Arrival/entering the classroom, attendance, transitions between classroom activities, bathroom breaks, participating in class discussions, and cooperative learning groups.

Teachers who frequently and consistently employ these types of routines are teaching and reinforcing their behavioral expectations.

Rules & Routines. Teach and demonstrate classroom rules and routines as specifically as you do academic content.

Teachers establish expectations through classroom rules and procedures, but also by communicating explicit learning goals. Students should know what is expected of them and how they will be assessed. Take time to teach students about your expectations and what you mean by those expectations. Take time to teach students the behaviors they expect students to use. Teachers must reinforce the behaviors and support students who use them.

Transitions: Use activities whenever moving from one activity or location throughout the center and grounds. This maintains the children attention and helps to keep them on track, while minimizing errant behaviors that occur when they are not constructively occupied. Choose different songs to use throughout the year to get from one activity to another. This helps to establish routines, so children know when to end, to get ready, to transition, and lets them know what activity will follow.

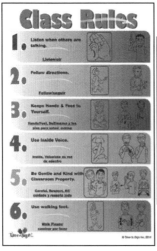

Quick Tip 2:
Establishing Caring Relationships

a. Student Familiarity. Get to know something personal about each student. Greet each one at the door to see how their day is going. If they are off to a rough start, you can correct things right then and there with a hug.

b. Knowing your children. Make it a point of knowing every student's name as quickly as possible, well enough to greet them outside of your normal classroom location. If students are going to trust and respect you, they need to know that you recognize them.

c. Student's needs. Students need love, acceptance, and consistency.

d. Believe in your students. Teachers should never 'give up' on any of their students. At this age it is of the utmost importance to work with children and their parents to correct behaviors.

e. Accomplishments. Be aware of students' accomplishments and provide positive reinforcement. Reinforce the effort not the accomplishment. It is crucial to let children know the importance of their continued diligence.

f. Family Communication. Send positive notes, phone calls, or emails home.

g. Sensitivity. Be sensitive to students' moods and concerns.

h. Praise. Praise more, criticize less.

i. Humor. Maintain a sense of humor.

j. Mutual Respect. Establish mutual respect between students, parents, and teachers.

k. Caring. Life has many difficult challenges for your students. You may be one of the few people that child believes cares about him or her. This could make difference in his or her life choices, or at least in his or her decision not to disrupt your class.

l. Behavior. Use all moments of questionable behavior as a teaching moment to insure the child knows the correct behavior.

m. Learn students' names and greet them at the door. A student who is having a bad day can be disarmed by the genuine concern of a teacher.

Your Favorite Teacher. Think about your favorite teacher as a child. They were not your favorite because they were the best instructors. They were your favorite because they cared about you.

Quick Tip 3:
Social-Emotional Learning (SEL)

a. Foundation of Positive Behavior. Social-emotional skills are a foundation for children's positive behavior in school. There are three broad areas of SEL: cognitive regulation/executive function, emotion processes, and interpersonal skills.

b. SEL Skills. Social-emotional skills needed by students include: knowing when to speak/listen, following directions, being able to work cooperatively within groups, alternatives to aggression, positive expression of emotions, dealing with feelings, dealing with stress, dealing with conflicts, negotiating interpersonal communication such as joining a group, working cooperatively with peers, convincing others of your point, exhibit self-control, display determination and perseverance, and planning skills including goal setting or decision making.

c. SEL Instruction. Three tenets of social skills instruction are as follows:

    i. All behaviors are learned; therefore, appropriate behaviors can be taught and learned by all students.

    ii. Social skills instruction should be customized to meet individual students' communication and behavioral needs.

    iii. The appropriate approach in teaching social skills includes: modeling, leading, reinforcing, practicing, and monitoring.

d.   SEL Skills Mastery Results. Children who are strong in these SEL skills are less disruptive and better able to learn from classroom instruction. Children who are lacking in these areas are more likely to be off-task, engage in conflicts with peers or adults, and minimize learning time for themselves and disrupt the learning of others.

e.   Teachers and SEL. It is not just for students. Teachers must use their SEL skills to establish high-quality relationships with students.

f.   Reframing Disruptive Behavior. Teachers should reframe disruptive behavior and other classroom management challenges.

g.   About SEL. Research indicates that lower order social-emotional skills emerge earlier than others and lay the foundation for more complex higher order skills.

Quick Tip 4:
Planning and Implementing Engaging Instruction

a. Instruction. Aspects of direct and explicit instruction include:
    i.   Stating expectations and objectives at the beginning of each lesson.
    ii. Presenting the information to the students using modeling and demonstration.
    iii. Use scaffolding, or prompting and prompt fading. Providing students with opportunities for practice.
b. Be caring, but resolutely serious in your instruction.
c. Project confidence and demonstrate that everything you ask of them has been deliberately planned in your students' best interest.
d. Student Involved Learning. Create highly engaging instruction by providing frequent opportunities for students to respond.
e. Materials. Have all materials organized and ready prior to the start of the lesson.
f. Student Attention. Establish an attention getting signal.
g. Adaptability. Adapt content and activities to students' interests and abilities.
h. Challenge Students. Ensure students work at the appropriate level of challenge or difficulty.
i. Autonomy & Choices. Provide opportunity to exercise autonomy and make choices.
j. Enthusiasm. Project enthusiasm for all activities taught to students.

k. Knowledge Transfer. Teachers should explain the applicability of what they instruct to other subjects.
l. Preparation. Being prepared allows you to be practice proper classroom management that is more likely to be thoughtful, concrete, consistent, and implemented in a calm and supportive way.
m. Peer Instruction & Collaboration. Use peer-facilitated instruction and collaboration.
n. Organize the Lesson.
o. Preparation is needed to develop an engaging lesson that moves smoothly forward and permits the teacher the opportunity to communicate with every child.
    i.   You should design your lesson plans with classroom management in mind.
    ii. Build teaching strategies and interventions into each lesson.
    iii. Develop one-on-one and small group strategies, allowing time for social interaction and reflection.
    iv. Organization also involves ample preparation time arranging handouts, preparing supplies, writing on the board and taking care of myriad other tasks.

    By preparing in advance, you can prevent gaps during the lesson when you lose students' attention and better manage your classroom.
p. Develop a series of activity transitions. By doing so going from one activity to another can be smooth, without losing their attention.

Quick Tip 5:
Classroom Management Techniques

a. Shaping Behavior. You need to be deliberate, to be assertive, and to always have a reason for everything.

b. Planned Ignoring. If an attention-seeking behavior, such as pencil tapping, is ignored, the child may first increase the intensity of the tapping but may eventually stop due to lack of reinforcement.

c. Signal Interference. Nonverbal signals, such as the use of sign language, and verbal signals, such as the reminder of the rules, can signal students to change their own behavior.

d. Proximity and Touch Control. The presence of the teacher nearby can remind students to refocus, refrain, and reengage.

e. Involvement in the Interest Relationship. Changing examples to reflect student interests or shifting the activity can reel students back into classroom discussions. Personal attention can also serve to reengage students.

f. Hurdle Help. Providing instructional support rather than a reprimand or redirect can sometimes help this situation.

g. Regrouping. Simply moving the players around can be an effective strategy for addressing unwanted behaviors. Teachers should take care to remove emotion from this strategy since negative attention can be reinforcing to some students.

h. Restructuring. Teachers can change an activity that is not going as planned in order to avoid or reduce undesired behaviors.

    i.   Supports that are embedded in the environment help students manage themselves by reinforcing expectations and promoting positive behavior even when the teacher is unavailable.

i. Documentation. Write down a bullet point snapshot on the incident immediately. Then come back and revisit once you have calmed down to amend and add more detail. Effective classroom management requires perpetual observation and documentation. Teachers need to continually assess their management strategies and adapt as needed. Documentation helps educators identify patterns and anticipate and correct recurring problems. Careful observation and documentation, meticulously writing down what has transpired (often done later), what was said, and what exactly happened lets teachers reflect upon and improve their interactions with students, as well as their overall classroom management plan.

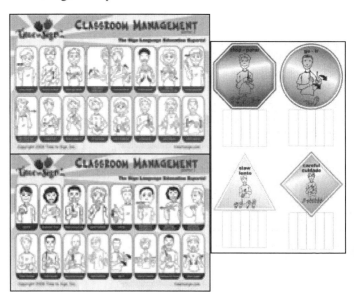

Quick Tip 6:
Addressing Discipline Issues

a. Classroom Climate. Studies show that teachers who had positive relationships with their students, had almost 1/3 fewer discipline problems and rule violations over the course of the year. Unlike teachers who did not have positive relationships with their students.

b. Non-verbal Interventions. Use nonverbal interventions such as proximity, eye contact, sign language, and facial expressions to redirect misbehavior.

c. Minor Misbehavior. Ignore minor misbehavior, if possible.

d. Verbal Interventions. Use brief, concise, and specific sign language and/or verbal interventions to redirect misbehavior.

e. Teacher Communication. A final way of communicating a strong teacher presence is to calmly, clearly, and consistently reinforce rules or expectations.

  i. Yelling, moving too close to students, lecturing, displaying strong emotion, and avoiding the offending student behavior communicate teacher insecurity.

  ii. A positive classroom climate communicates to students that the teacher is calm and confident in your ability to respond to student needs; either by reinforcing the rules, redirecting misbehavior, or addressing an extreme situation.

f. Positive Language. Use positive teacher language,
    and sign language, to tell the child what to do
    rather than what not to do.

g. Student Engagement. If students are engaged,
    classroom management issues are greatly
    reduced.

h. Patience. Patience on the part of the teacher is
    key. The teacher must react calmly, but with a
    firm voice.

i. Teachable Moment. All occasions of misbehavior
    should be looked upon as teachable moments to
    correct misbehavior and advise children of the
    appropriate alternative.

Quick Tip 7:
Self-Regulation for
Children's Instruction

Self-regulation and determination/ perseverance are the two skills that kindergarten teachers say are most needed to be successful as our preschoolers advance.

Teaching children to begin to internally monitor specific negative behaviors they exhibit can be the first step to eliminating these behaviors.

Children's self-monitoring interventions include the following steps:

a. Identifying Errant Behavior. Identification of a specific errant behavior.
b. Student Buy-in. Soliciting buy-in from the student on the advantages of self-monitoring to help eliminate the specific behavior.
c. Role-playing. Use specific instances to role-play and teach your preschoolers appropriate behaviors, the use of manners, and the necessary social and emotional skills:

i. Self-management. Managing emotions and behaviors to achieve one's goals.

ii. Self-awareness. Recognizing one's emotions and values as well as one's strengths and challenges.

iii. Social awareness. Showing understanding and empathy for others.

iv. Responsible decision-making. Making ethical, constructive choices about personal and social behavior.

v. Relationship skills. Forming positive relationships, working in teams, dealing effectively with conflict.

d. Data. Developing a method for monitoring and collecting data on the behavior.

e. Teacher Monitoring. Correction of the behavior, over time, with concurrent reduction and ultimately eliminating of teacher monitoring.

f. Self-regulation. Teaching the student to self-monitor and helping with reminders when target behavior occurs.

Quick Tip 8:
Knowing & Supporting Your Students

a. Strategies to Enhance Climate. Simple strategies such as proximity, eye contact, or the incorporation of students' names or interests during instruction can contribute to an overall positive classroom climate.

b. Support to Meet Expectations. Given proper instruction, motivation, and control, students will meet our high expectations for them.

c. Knowing Students. Learning more about students' lives outside of the classroom will go a long way toward successful interactions with students within classrooms. Knowing about the significant people in students' lives will give teachers insight as to the important adults to involve in the support of their education, which in turn will provide needed information about whom to seek support from when the student is in need.

d. Community. Teachers should make a point of understanding the community from which their student's come.

e. Family Involvement. Teachers and the school must actively involve families in the education of students.

   i. To encourage family involvement, all family members should feel valued and welcome in the classroom and school.

   ii. Teachers should maintain family communication with a frequency based on student need and family desire.

f. Teachers and Staff as a Resource. While the classroom teacher is not a social worker and therefore does not have responsibility or the ability to solve all of the problems families may face. However, they can serve as a trusted point person who is aware of community resources to direct families to needed services.

g. Expectations. Set high expectations for your students. The higher the expectations the greater the social, emotional, and academic growth.

h. Relationships and Classroom Management. Teachers who establish and maintain positive, trusting relationships with students can use their history of positive inter actions in order to address challenges as they develop.

i. Teacher-Student Relationships. High-quality teacher-student relationships are characterized by caring and openness to student needs on one hand and by clear boundaries and consistent consequences on the other hand. The trick is finding the right balance.

Quick Tip 9:
Encouraging Helpful Hands

a. Student help. Students feel invested when they assist the teacher in the classroom. It also builds their self-esteem.

b. Teach children to care. Develop a small garden and have the children help in maintaining it. Teach signs to ask questions it is a great way to connect. Teach children to work together to build relationship and keep a journal of garden's progress.

c. Helping Activities. Students to help getting supplies, passing out papers, or straighten the room.

d. Avoid Favoritism. You should be careful to let everyone help to avoid favoritism.

e. Learn the basic 6 Children Communication Languages and assign roles based on them. Who is your speaker, quality time, helper, encourager, hugger, and artist/gifter.

f. Engage the children in activities to help one another and assign buddy help as needed.

Garden Signs:

WATER   **GARDEN**   **DIRT**

PLANT/GROW   *FRUIT*   *VEGETABLES*

Quick Tip 10:
Organizing the Classroom Layout

a. Clutter. Purge your classroom of all unwanted clutter.
b. Personalize your classroom. Personalize the classroom, so that it communicates information about you and your students.
c. Establish learning centers. Create learning centers such as dramatic play, puzzles, blocks, kitchen play, reading, and transportation.
d. Develop a number and name system that assigns each child a number. Label their mat, cubbie, and other personal items with their name and number, so there is no confusion amongst the children and what belongs to whom. The children can use their Velcro number/name card to check into a learning center to limit the number of children at each to the desired amount.
e. Materials storage. Make it clear where classroom materials belong, so children can self-monitor in the process of clean-up. Posting a picture of what originally went there is helpful.

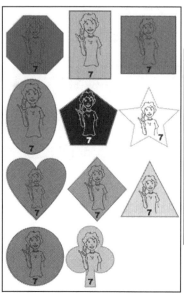

Early Childhood Social and Emotional Patterns

The Speaker
Patterns: The speaker loves to talk to others, and learns through communication.
Maximizing Learning: Dedicate time to listening to them, have them communicate class instructions to others, and allow them to verbally participate in circle time and other activities.

speak   person

The Helper
Patterns: The helper loves to serve others.
Maximizing Learning: Have them assist with setup, cleanup, and leading of activities; have them buddy with new, shy, or special needs students; have them run errands in class; and give them verbal and visual praise daily.

help   person

The Time Keeper
Patterns: The time keeper loves spending time in the company of others.
Maximizing Learning: Have them participate in group activities, give them individual attention to reinforce their learning and behavior, take walks as a group, and give the gift of yourself, your time.

value   time   person

The Gifter
Patterns: The gifter loves to make and bring things to others.
Maximizing Learning: Have them make daily art projects to take home to family, give verbal praise daily, give them thoughtful personalized gifts, and give the gift of your presence.

gift   person

The Hugger
Patterns: The hugger loves to give and receive affection, and engage in physical touch (hug, pat on the back, high fives, etc.).
Maximizing Learning: Greet and say goodbye daily with a positive touches, hug, pat on the back, high fives, and holding hands.

hug   person

The Encourager
Patterns: The encourager loves to give and receive compliments and praise.
Maximizing Learning: Pair with shy or new student, provide words of affirmation and appreciation, use kind and encouraging words in daily praise, and write notes of encouragement.

words   encourage   person

To order additional Time to Sign products
please visit our web-site
www.TimeToSign.com
or call (321) 726-9466

Michael & Lillian Hubler

ABOUT THE AUTHORS

Dr. Michael S. Hubler (Ed.D.) and his wife Lillian Hubler founded Time to Sign, Inc. in 2000. The company was founded because the they recognized the benefits of using American Sign Language (ASL) with their children; and then with other children, families, educators, and care givers around the world. Time to Sign programs have been used in Family Childcares, Private Preschools, Early Head Start, Head Start, and School Districts.

Lillian is a nationally acclaimed presenter /trainer. Since 2000, she has trained over 50,000 educators, parents and children around the world in age appropriate and developmentally appropriate sign language usage. She is renowned for her high energy workshops and presentations. She has appeared on CNN, ABC, NBC, as well as having been interviewed by Florida Today and the Washington Post.

Dr. Michael S. Hubler (Ed.D.) is the Director of Educational Curriculum and Product Development for Time to Sign. He is has a Ed.D. in the field of education, specializing in the positive impacts of sign language on social and emotional development. Dr. Hubler has served as an executive director for various educational and community services organizations, specializing in services and programs to enhance the education, personal growth, and development of at-risk children.

Michael and Lillian are also former owners of a licensed day care with 135 children from birth to 12 years of age. They have written over 35 sign language books including preschool and school-age curriculums. Time to Sign's trainings and materials are uniquely designed to promote social emotional development and reduce children's challenging behavior in social settings. Their training programs and materials also promote literacy, language development, and communication.

Made in the USA
Columbia, SC
01 October 2023